Earth's Wate

by Kira Freed

Table of Contents

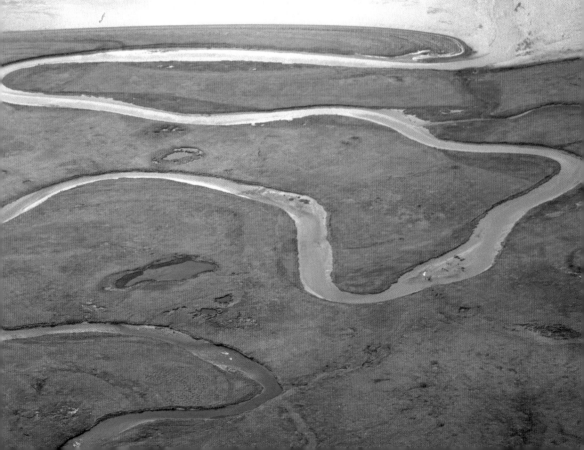

I need to know these words.

condensation

evaporation

groundwater

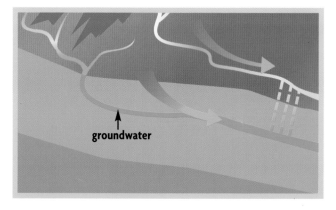

groundwater

precipitation

water cycle

water vapor

3

What Is the Water Cycle?

The **water cycle** is a pattern in nature. The water cycle is happening all the time. Earth has huge amounts of water. This water is always moving.

The water cycle moves Earth's water to different places. Water changes form as it moves.

Did You Know?
Water is matter. Matter has three forms:
- liquid
- solid
- gas

▲ the water cycle

One part of the water cycle is **evaporation**. Evaporation happens when the sun warms liquid water. Then the water changes form. The liquid water becomes gas. This gas is **water vapor**.

We cannot see water vapor. We can feel water vapor on some hot days. Air feels damp because it holds large amounts of water vapor.

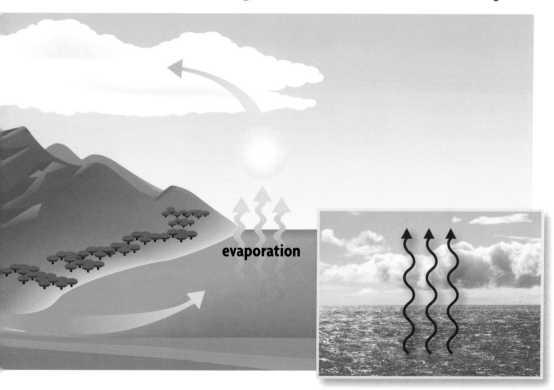

evaporation

▲ evaporation

The next part of the water cycle is **condensation**. The water vapor rises into higher, cooler air. The cooler air cannot hold large amounts of water vapor. Some of the water vapor becomes liquid again. Then clouds form.

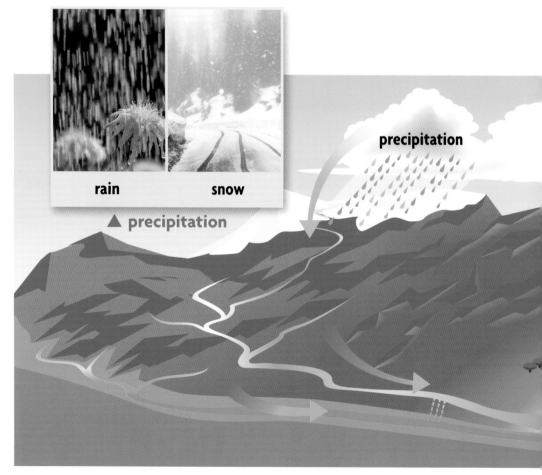

rain   snow

▲ precipitation

precipitation

The clouds become heavy with water. Clouds cannot hold all the water. The water becomes **precipitation**. Precipitation is the next part of the water cycle.

Precipitation is water that falls from clouds. The water falls to the ground. The water can fall in different forms.

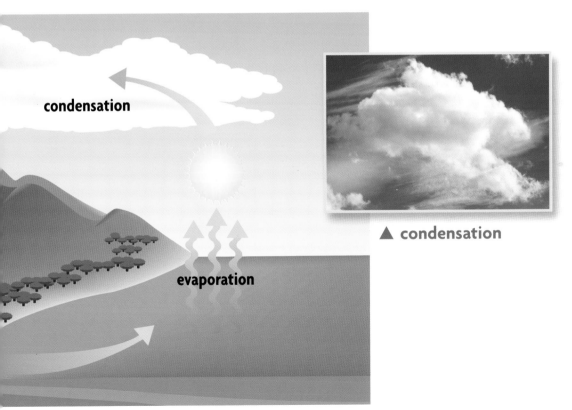

condensation

evaporation

▲ condensation

Then some precipitation seeps, or goes slowly, into the ground. This water becomes **groundwater**. The groundwater flows between soil and rocks. Some groundwater collects deep under the ground.

Some precipitation stays on the ground. This water is surface water. Surface water flows into streams and rivers. Next, streams and rivers flow into lakes and oceans. Then evaporation happens to this water again.

▲ surface water

surface water

seeping water

groundwater

Frozen precipitation is ice. Ice is another form of water. Ice is a solid.

Earth has ice in cold places. The sun warms some of the ice. The heat from the sun causes this ice to melt. The ice becomes liquid water. Some water seeps into the ground and becomes groundwater. Some water flows into rivers, lakes, and oceans.

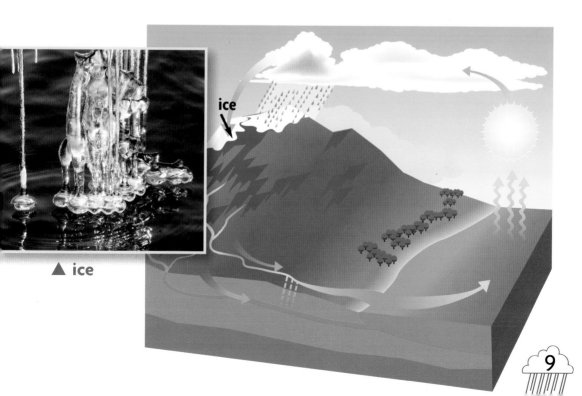

ice

▲ ice

Where Is Earth's Water?

Earth's water is always moving through the water cycle. Some of the water is liquid. Other water is gas or solid.

Imagine a drop of water. Imagine this drop traveling through the water cycle. The drop changes form many times.

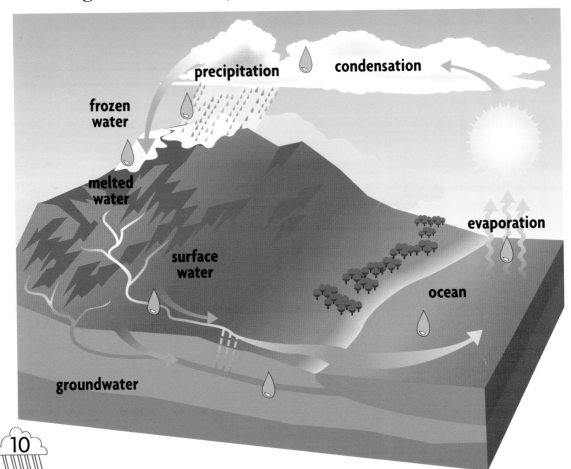

Most of Earth's water is liquid. Earth's oceans hold large amounts of water. Oceans cover more than three-fourths of Earth. Land covers less than one-fourth of Earth. The oceans hold almost all the water on Earth. The water in oceans is salt water.

◀ Earth's oceans are blue on these globes.

▲ Salt water is in oceans.

Water is also in rivers and streams. Lakes and ponds have water, too. This water is fresh water. Fresh water comes from rain and snow.

Fresh water is different from salt water. Most animals that live on land need fresh water. Their bodies cannot use salt water.

Did You Know?
The Amazon River has more water than any other river. The Amazon River is in South America.

The Amazon River

▲ Rivers and streams have fresh water.

Some of Earth's water is ice. The South Pole has large sheets of ice. Ice floats in cold oceans. Tall mountains have ice, too.

Some of Earth's water is water vapor. The air around Earth has water vapor.

▲ This mountain has ice and snow all year.

◀ This ice is at the South Pole.

How Does the Water Cycle Cause Weather?

The water cycle helps make weather. Earth has many types of weather. Storms happen on some days. The sky is blue on other days. Sometimes clouds cover the sky.

The sun heats Earth's surface. Some parts of Earth's surface get more heat than other parts. The different amounts of heat cause wind.

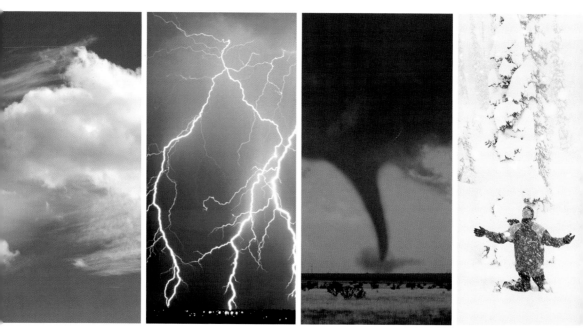

▲ The water cycle helps produce different types of weather.

14

Wind is part of the weather. The sun causes wind by warming the air. Then the hot air rises. Cold air moves where the warm air was. Wind happens because cold air follows hot air.

3. Hot air cools.

2. Hot air rises.

4. Cold air sinks.

1. Cold air warms.

▲ Air of different temperatures makes wind.

Clouds are part of the weather, too. Condensation causes clouds.

Hot air carries water vapor high into the sky. Then condensation causes some water vapor to become liquid again. Tiny drops of water group together and become clouds.

Some Types of Clouds		
Cloud	**Name of Cloud**	**Type of Weather**
	Cumulus	nice weather
	Cirrus	weather that will change soon
	Stratus	cloudy

Sometimes precipitation falls from clouds. Precipitation falls because clouds get too heavy with water.

Earth has different types of precipitation. Water can fall as rain or snow. Sometimes ice falls from clouds.

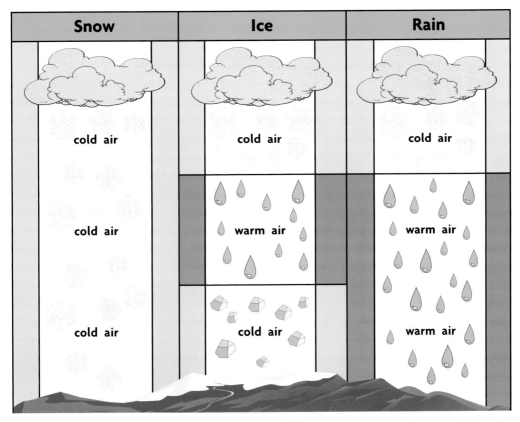

Snow	Ice	Rain
cold air	cold air	cold air
cold air	warm air	warm air
cold air	cold air	warm air

▲ Different temperatures cause different types of precipitation.

Storms are wild weather. The water cycle causes many types of storms.

The most common storms have rain. Sometimes hot air holds large amounts of water vapor. This damp air rises very quickly. Huge clouds form from condensation. Then rain storms can happen. Precipitation falls as a result.

Did You Know?

Too much rain can cause floods. Snow and ice that melt can cause floods, too. The water fills rivers to the top. No more water can seep into the ground. The water flows onto land.

▲ Water covers land during a flood.

▲ Lightning happens during some storms.

The water cycle causes other types of storms, too. Some storms bring large amounts of snow. Rain freezes during other storms. Different storms happen in different seasons.

Earth's water is always moving. Water is always changing form, too. The water cycle causes different weather around the world.

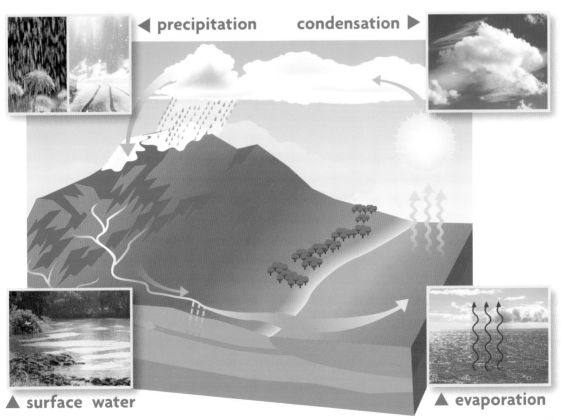

◀ precipitation   condensation ▶

▲ surface water   ▲ evaporation

Glossary

condensation
(kahn-den-SAY-shun):
**when water vapor
changes to liquid**
See page 6.

evaporation
(ih-va-puh-RAY-shun):
**when water changes
to gas**
See page 5.

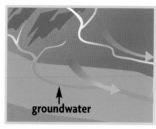

groundwater
(GROWND-WAU-ter):
water in the ground
See page 8.

precipitation
(prih-sih-puh-TAY-shun):
**water that falls
from clouds**
See page 7.

water cycle
(WAU-ter SY-kul): **all
the ways water moves
and changes form**
See page 4.

water vapor
(WAU-ter VAY-per):
**water that is gas
in the air**
See page 5.

Index